ACT
NOW!

31 Nuggets to Activate, Cultivate and Transform Your World

Praise for ACT NOW!

"The Word of God never changes. But in every season, God raises up new voices to illumine God's eternal Word and thereby to help us all fulfill the destiny that He has for our lives. My friend, Pamela Hardy, is one of today's important new voices, and her outstanding devotional, *ACT NOW!* will take you to a higher level in allowing God's blessings to flow into you and through you to others!"

C. Peter Wagner
Vice-President
Global Spheres, Inc.

"Old mindsets limit the potential that God has placed within His people. Wrong and often negative thoughts captivate a person and prevent the person from attaining God's plan for their future. Pamela Hardy has written a powerful devotional to break the old cycle of debilitating thoughts. *ACT NOW!* is designed to take you on a life transforming journey. I recommend this book for anyone desiring to break out of old destructive thoughts and enter a new way of thinking and living. You will never be the same after implementing the nuggets found in *ACT NOW!*"

Barbara Wentroble
President: International Breakthrough Ministries
President: Business Owners for Christ International
Author: *Empowered for Your Purpose*;
Prophetic Intercession; *Praying With Authority*;
Fighting for Your Prophetic Promises;
Removing the Veil of Deception

"Dr. Pamela Hardy is a visionary worshipper who dances to the sound of God's heartbeat. Her daily devotional, *ACT NOW! 31 Nuggets to Activate, Cultivate and Transform Your World*, will help you to spiritually align and march in a new way with God's divine plans for your life. The Scriptures she has chosen and the activations she has developed will renew your mind to think higher thoughts. She will compel you to take Godly actions to facilitate changes that will advance your life into a broader sphere of prosperity."

Dr. Barbie L. Breathitt
Author: *Dream Encounter, Dream Seer,*
Gateway to the Seer Realm
and *Dream Interpreter*
Breath of the Spirit Ministries

"The promises of God are from everlasting to everlasting! Who then, would not be willing to hear a word from the Lord daily? Your day can gain a lifetime of confidence that can change your mindset from worry, being frantic, depression, anger, rage, anxiety and other forms of dismay by reading one of these nuggets only once a day. Please join me as we fill our hearts with chunks of spiritual nuggets from a river that will never run dry."

Rev. Dr. Thelma Wells (Mama T),
CEO,
That A Girl & Friends
Speakers Agency and Enrichment Tours

ACT NOW!

31 Nuggets to Activate, Cultivate and Transform Your World

PAMELA HARDY

BASAR PUBLISHING

ACT NOW! 31 Nuggets to Activate, Cultivate and Transform Your World

© 2015 by Pamela Hardy

All Scripture quotations, unless otherwise indicated, are taken from the King James Bible Version.

ISBN: 978-1-942013-45-7

Printed in the United States of America.

Cover Design: Eric Culberson

Editors: Rekesha Pittman, ShaVonne Thomas

TABLE OF CONTENTS

Introduction
Nugget 1 - Yesterday is Gone.
Nugget 2 - God's Grace is Sufficient.
Nugget 3 - You Were Already Forgiven.
Nugget 4 - The Secret to Your Future.
Nugget 5 - You Can Always Trust in God.
Nugget 6 - God Hears You.
Nugget 7 - You Have Passed From Death to Life.
Nugget 8 - God Wants to Bless You.
Nugget 9 - You Have Been Called To Live Beyond the Ordinary.
Nugget 10 - Step Into the Destiny God Has for You.
Nugget 11 - You Are Called to Advance the Kingdom of Heaven.
Nugget 12 - God Wants to Enlarge Your Borders.
Nugget 13 - You Are Prophetic.
Nugget 14 - You Can Live a Life of Revelation.
Nugget 15 - You Are Complete in Him.
Nugget 16 - You Are Dead, Yet Alive!
Nugget 17 - You Are a Sharp Instrument in the Hand of the
          Lord.
Nugget 18 - You Were Made for Glory.
Nugget 19 - You Can Expect the Unexpected!
Nugget 20 - God Will Open New Doors for You.
Nugget 21 - God's Love Lives in You.
Nugget 22 - You Are Resilient.
Nugget 23 - You Are Led by the Spirit of God.
Nugget 24 - You Can Have a Renewed Spirit.
Nugget 25 - God Has a Restoration of All Things for You.
Nugget 26 - You Are Filled with CHAYIL Power.
Nugget 27 - The Throne Attitude is Yours!
Nugget 28 - You Are a Force in the Earth!
Nugget 29 - If You Can See It, You Can Have It!
Nugget 30 - You Are Anointed to Fulfill a Specific Purpose in God's
          Plan.
Nugget 31 - You Can Have the Wisdom of God.

Welcome to the Journey!

ACT NOW! 31 Nuggets to Activate, Cultivate and Transform Your World is a daily devotional journal to help you change the way you think. When your thoughts line up with God's Word, your world will change and be transformed.

A nugget is defined as a small lump of gold or other precious metal. Psalm 19:7-11 says:

Psalm 19:7-11

7 The law of the LORD is perfect, converting the soul: the testimony of the LORD is sure, making wise the simple.

8 The statutes of the LORD are right, rejoicing the heart: the commandment of the LORD is pure, enlightening the eyes.

9 The fear of the LORD is clean, enduring for ever: the judgments of the LORD are true and righteous altogether.

10 More to be desired are they than gold, yea, than much fine gold: sweeter also than honey and the honeycomb.

11 Moreover by them is thy servant warned: and in keeping of them there is great reward.

Verse 9 says God's word is be desired more than gold. This speaks to the purity of God's word, meaning it has the ability to refine us and purify us, thereby bringing out the absolute best God has for us.

A nugget is also a valuable idea or fact. God's word is true. It's a valuable fact that reveals His righteousness.

ACT!

Activate. To make active or operative, to energize.

Cultivate. To break up soil in preparation for sowing or planting.

Transform. To make a thorough or dramatic change in the form, appearance, or character of.

NOW! At the present moment in time; currently; right away; immediately; instantly; promptly; without delay; as soon as possible; ASAP.

Philippians 4:6-9
6 Be careful for nothing; but in every thing by prayer and supplication with thanksgiving let your requests be made known unto God.
7 And the peace of God, which passeth all understanding, shall keep your hearts and minds through Christ Jesus.
8 Finally, brethren, whatsoever things are true, whatsoever things are honest, whatsoever things are just, whatsoever things are pure, whatsoever things are lovely, whatsoever things are of good report; if there be any virtue, and if there be any praise, think on these things.

9 Those things, which ye have both learned, and received, and heard, and seen in me, do: and the God of peace shall be with you.

Verse 8 tells us to think on these things. The word think means to take an inventory.

Over the next 31 days, I encourage you to take an inventory of where you are—from your thought processes to your relationships, expectations and hopes for the future. Transformation will cause you to overcome.

God wants to do a new thing in you. As you meditate daily on each of the nuggets, be confident that the "new thing" is not only being formed in you, but your "new thing" is being formed as a pathway on which you can walk. Your thoughts will shift into a new place. Your life will shift into a new place. Your language will shift into a new place. Your expectations will shift into a new place.

The new place is waiting for you. Can you not see it? If you choose the "new" everyday, you will receive revelation beyond your ability to comprehend. You will see it because there will be a manifestation. Once His glory manifests, everything changes. Right now, God is releasing to you His grace for your new place!

Each day, take time to allow Holy Spirit to speak to your heart about each scripture. You have a voice, so speak each daily activation out loud to release cultivation that brings transformation. Repeat the prayer several times throughout the day. By doing this daily, you will activate, cultivate and transform your world. In Joshua 1:8, God instructed him to meditate on the Word day and night so he could make his way prosperous and have good success. The word meditate means to murmur, to mutter, to speak, to talk or to utter.

Your words are seeds. Be careful what you say. You will produce what you speak. The blessing is in the instructions. Stay focused. Be diligent. God will watch over His Word to perform it and you will experience the difference the next 31 days will make!

Joshua 1:7-9
7 Only be thou strong and very courageous, that thou mayest observe to do according to all the law, which Moses my servant commanded thee: turn not from it to the right hand or to the left, that thou mayest prosper whithersoever thou goest.
8 This book of the law shall not depart out of thy mouth; but thou shalt meditate therein day and night, that thou mayest observe to do according to all that is written therein: for then thou shalt make thy way prosperous, and then thou shalt have good success.
9 Have not I commanded thee? Be strong and of a good courage; be not afraid, neither be thou dismayed: for the LORD thy God is with thee whithersoever thou goest.

Your Nugget for Today - 1

Yesterday is Gone

ACT NOW! Yesterday is gone. You cannot change it. We have to live for today. He gives us strength for each new day. Move forward into His plans! Great is His love for you. His plans, desires and thoughts for you is to love and to be loved. Your future is abundant and bright.

Regret is defined as disappointment over something that has happened or been done, especially a loss or missed opportunity. Regret can keep you from the fullness of that future. Release all regrets to God. Regret is any unresolved past issue that will fester in your soul if ignored. Regret can cause you to be frozen in the past and can keep you from freely living in the present. It can zap your strength, blind you to the purposes of God and hold you emotionally captive. Don't allow yourself to be lost in the maze of regret. Regret is not from the heart of your Father so release it all to Him right now. Let nothing stand in the way.

Run into the abundant life God has for you! Abundant life means abundant in quantity and superior in quality. Let God give you vision that creates faith for your abundant, bright future. Allow Him to prepare and equip you for your next season so you can go forward with fresh manna and a new anointing.

Scripture Activation

Jeremiah 29:11-14

11 For I know the thoughts that I think toward you, saith the LORD, thoughts of peace, and not of evil, to give you an expected end.

12 Then shall ye call upon me, and ye shall go and pray unto me, and I will hearken unto you.

13 And ye shall seek me, and find me, when ye shall search for me with all your heart.

14 And I will be found of you, saith the LORD: and I will turn away your captivity, and I will gather you from all the nations, and from all the places whither I have driven you, saith the LORD; and I will bring you again into the place whence I caused you to be carried away captive.

<u>My prayer to activate, cultivate and transform my world:</u>

"Father, yesterday is gone. I cannot change it. I will live for You today. I will move forward into Your plans for my life. Thank You that the thoughts You think toward me are thoughts of peace and not evil. You have an expected end for me. I release all regret to You right now! Your Word says You have abundant, quality life for me! I receive it! Prepare and equip me for my next season so I can go forward with fresh manna and a new anointing. My future is bright! Thank You for turning my captivity!"

Your Nugget for Today - 2

God's Grace is Sufficient

ACT NOW! God's grace is sufficient! It's enough! God, Who cannot lie, promises such amazing, never-ending, all-sufficient grace. It's His grace that makes us strong in the power of His might. It's His power and might, not ours.

His grace, power and might rests upon us like a tent or tabernacle that provides shelter and rest. His grace allows our ordinary abilities to be transformed by Holy Spirit, living in us to rule and reign in our hearts, thoughts and words. The Bible tells us that both grace and truth are realized in and through Jesus Christ. Truth is defined as that which is in accordance with facts or reality. So truth is reality. Truth brings freedom. God only operates in truth. All of His works are done in truth. He answers those who call upon Him in truth. That's the realm and the domain that He operates in.

Freedom is experienced as you live in the reality of His truth. Live in truth so you can be free to be uniquely you. The truth is that God alone is full of grace and truth. God is faithful and boundless in His grace and truth. His grace is timeless. His truth endures forever. Live in His truth, trust in His saving grace.

Scripture Activation

Ephesians 2:4-9

4 But God, who is rich in mercy, for his great love wherewith he loved us,

5 Even when we were dead in sins, hath quickened us together with Christ, (by grace ye are saved;)

6 And hath raised us up together, and made us sit together in heavenly places in Christ Jesus:

7 That in the ages to come he might shew the exceeding riches of his grace in his kindness toward us through Christ Jesus.

8 For by grace are ye saved through faith; and that not of yourselves: it is the gift of God:

9 Not of works, lest any man should boast.

<u>My prayer to activate, cultivate and transform my world:</u>

"Father, thank You that Your grace is enough for me! Where would I be without Your grace? Thank You that Your grace rests upon me today. Fill me with continued revelation of Your grace. You are a God of truth. Thank You that I experience Your freedom as I live in the reality of Your truth. You are faithful and boundless in Your grace and truth. Thank You for Your amazing grace and Your enduring truth."

Your Nugget for Today - 3

You Were Already Forgiven

ACT NOW! You were already forgiven, loved and chosen from before the foundation of the world! The word chosen means to be favored. It means to be hand-picked. The God of your salvation, gives you strength and exceeding joy. Not only does He favor you, He loves you with an everlasting love.

Today, purpose to spend time in His presence, having a heart of worship because He who first loved you is worthy. Let not your time with the Lord be just a time of self-pity, self-survival or self-preservation. When you realize that you were forgiven, loved and chosen from before the foundation of the world, perfect love will come to cast out all fear. Any feelings of inadequacy will disappear. You will begin to see from God's perspective and His peace will replace all anxiety.

No matter what others may say to you, no matter how others may treat you and no matter what things may look like, rejoice in His love! Forgive yourself! Be confident that the One who has favored you and chosen you, also hears you, sees you and daily draws you to Himself. Rest assured. Only believe. You are favored, hand-picked, forgiven, loved and chosen.

ACT NOW!

Scripture Activation

Ephesians 1:2-4

2 Grace be to you, and peace, from God our Father, and from the Lord Jesus Christ.

3 Blessed be the God and Father of our Lord Jesus Christ, who hath blessed us with all spiritual blessings in heavenly places in Christ:

4 According as he hath chosen us in him before the foundation of the world, that we should be holy and without blame before him in love:

<u>My prayer to activate, cultivate and transform my world:</u>

"Father, thank You for loving me and for choosing me. I receive Your love. Let me see all things from Your eternal perspective and live each moment of each day in Your strength. I fix my eyes on You, keep my mind stayed on You and place my heart in Your hands."

The Secret to Your Future

ACT NOW! The secret to your future is hidden in your daily routine. The most valuable thing we can do with our lives is to spend time with God, the One who designed and created us. As we do this, He will show us the desires He has for us. Then we can begin to set goals based on faith because revelation will come from the heart of God. We can identify time wasters and move from stagnation to productivity.

Refuse to put anything in front of you that doesn't belong in your future. Refuse to feed what is not producing fruit. It no longer needs to live. Stay focused so you can discern the Lord's presence in the practical activities of everyday life. Prepare for your future by being disciplined, dedicated and committed to the plans and purposes of God. Discipline, dedication and commitment will define your gift.

God will not require anything from you that He did not already put in you. Since God does not change, that means you have to. The war is over your call and your destiny. You have a portion to secure! Determine now what you will do once you secure your inheritance. Choose to become a wise steward of His gifts. Daily commit your ways to Him and He will bring you into wide open places of blessings. Your future depends on your present. Ask the Lord to help you to seek Him so you can see Him each day. Let your daily routine will give birth to your future.

Scripture Activation

Proverbs 8:34-35

34 Blessed is the man that heareth me, watching daily at my gates, waiting at the posts of my doors.

35 For whoso findeth me findeth life, and shall obtain favour of the **LORD**.

<u>My prayer to activate, cultivate and transform my world:</u>

"Father, I thank You that as I watch daily at Your gates, I will find life and walk in favor! I lay down any activity not connected to my future. I will stay focused so I can discern Your presence and walk joyfully into my future."

Your Nugget for Today - 5

You Can Always Trust in God

ACT NOW! You can always trust in God. He will never leave you, nor will He forsake you. When I first came to believe in Christ, someone said to me, "People may fail you, but God never will." I have found that to be a very true statement. He can't fail you. It's against His very nature.

When you place your trust in Him, you are blessed. Trust Him in all things. Run to Him for protection. Confide in Him. Make the Lord your refuge. Trust can be broken when we feel disappointed. When others don't meet our expectations, we lose trust in their word. Put your trust in the only One who is able to keep His promises and provide a table in the wilderness of your heartache, your broken dreams or your own disobedience.

Trust in the only One who promises to keep you in the midst of what may seem like a dark situation. The darkness is not dark to the Lord. He sees through all of our "night" seasons. Even when you can't see His hand or feel His heart, He is there. So make the Lord your trust. Be confident, bold and secure in Him. Have full assurance of faith that He will always be your shelter and your strong tower.

Scripture Activation

Psalm 40:1-5

1 To the chief Musician, A Psalm of David. I waited patiently for the LORD; and he inclined unto me, and heard my cry.

2 He brought me up also out of an horrible pit, out of the miry clay, and set my feet upon a rock, and established my goings.

3 And he hath put a new song in my mouth, even praise unto our God: many shall see it, and fear, and shall trust in the LORD.

4 Blessed is that man that maketh the LORD his trust, and respecteth not the proud, nor such as turn aside to lies.

5 Many, O LORD my God, are thy wonderful works which thou hast done, and thy thoughts which are to us-ward: they cannot be reckoned up in order unto thee: if I would declare and speak of them, they are more than can be numbered.

<u>My prayer to activate, cultivate and transform my world:</u>

"Father, You are wonderful! Thank You for being trustworthy. You cannot lie. You cannot fail. I place my trust in You at all times. You are my refuge and my safe place. I am confident, bold and secure in You. I have full assurance of faith that You will always be my shelter and my strong tower. I praise Your name!"

14

ACT NOW!

Your Nugget for Today - 6

God Hears You

ACT NOW! God hears you and will not forsake you. In fact, God has rivers of refreshing for you, streams that will make you glad. In places that have been barren, God will release waters that will produce life. In places of despair or loss, His springs of living water will wash away all debris. Let Him show you how the desert places will become pools of living water. Parched ground will no longer be.

God will supernaturally pour His flood waters—waters to swim in. He will refresh and restore. No longer will you dig wells without water. Your thirst will be satisfied. You will be filled to overflowing with a revelation of His grace. It will not only fill you, but lift you higher and higher and carry you into new spiritual realms. Drink in deep.

Be filled with thanksgiving because the fight is fixed! God knows your end from the beginning. If you keep in mind that the battle is not yours, you can know without a doubt that you have victory in all things. So learn to do battle according to His instructions. WORSHIP only Him, WAIT in His presence until He gives you the WORD to use in the WARFARE against the enemy. Warfare simply means strategy and since Jesus already triumphed over the enemy, He alone is well able to give you the strategy you need to see your victory!

Scripture Activation

Isaiah 41:17-20

17 When the poor and needy seek water, and there is none, and their tongue faileth for thirst, I the LORD will hear them, I the God of Israel will not forsake them.

18 I will open rivers in high places, and fountains in the midst of the valleys: I will make the wilderness a pool of water, and the dry land springs of water.

19 I will plant in the wilderness the cedar, the shittah tree, and the myrtle, and the oil tree; I will set in the desert the fir tree, and the pine, and the box tree together:

20 That they may see, and know, and consider, and understand together, that the hand of the LORD hath done this, and the Holy One of Israel hath created it.

<u>My prayer to activate, cultivate and transform my world:</u>

"Father, thank You that You hear me and You will never forsake me. You satisfy me! Your rivers of refreshing water are mine and I drink deeply! Supernaturally pour Your flood waters over me that I may be refreshed and restored. Thank You that You already conquered sin and death and won the victory for me! I have victory in all things! The fight is fixed and I win!"

ACT NOW!

Your Nugget for Today - 7

You Have Passed From Death to Life

ACT NOW! You have passed from death to life! When you hear God's voice and believe His Word, you become free from condemnation. You are free to rise up and live the resurrection life. You no longer live in bondage to death or the fear of death. You have passed from sin and death to life and peace. You have passed from being separated from God to being an heir with Jesus Christ of all that is eternal.

Your future passes from death to life. Your thoughts pass from death to life. Your emotions pass from death to life. Your expectations pass from death to life. Your relationships pass from death to life. Your desires pass from death to life. Your finances pass from death to life.

The winds of life are blowing over you now, creating visible changes. Be fully persuaded! Be overwhelmed with this truth. You have crossed over! You have passed from failure to success, from grief to joy, from fear to faith, from victim to victor. You have passed from death to life! Now allow Him to rule and reign in your heart.

17

Scripture Activation

John 5:24-26

24 Verily, verily, I say unto you, He that heareth my word, and believeth on him that sent me, hath everlasting life, and shall not come into condemnation; but is passed from death unto life.

25 Verily, verily, I say unto you, The hour is coming, and now is, when the dead shall hear the voice of the Son of God: and they that hear shall live.

26 For as the Father hath life in himself; so hath he given to the Son to have life in himself

---

<u>My prayer to activate, cultivate and transform my world:</u>

"Father, I thank You that I am completely free! I command resurrection life to arise in me. I overcome all situations and circumstances because every part of my life has been surrendered to the life of Christ. I have already passed from death to life!"

18

Your Nugget for Today - 8

God Wants to Bless You

ACT NOW! God wants to bless you more and more each day! God is a God of increase and multiplication. You are His child so His desire is for you to increase and multiply.

Look back at your life and see how God has always provided. Now look at where you are today and see the increase He has already brought in your life. He increases our strength. He increases our wisdom. He increases our resources. He increases our peace. He increases our finances. He increases our joy. He increases us in all things.

As you diligently seek Him, He will reward you and cause you to increase and prosper in every area—spiritually, relationally, creatively, physically, financially and in your occupation. Take time to inventory each area of your life and ask the Lord what you can do to bring increase. Then whatever He says, do it!

Obedience is always the key to unlock any door. The person of Jesus Christ brings peace and the principles of Jesus Christ will cause us to flourish. The Lord will not only bless you and increase you, but He will bring increase and blessings to your children. Right now, break every strategy of the enemy and receive an abundance of revelation that leads to spiritual rewards, increase and multiplication.

Scripture Activation

Psalm 115:14-16

14 The **LORD** shall increase you more and more, you and your children.

15 Ye are blessed of the **LORD** which made heaven and earth.

16 The heaven, even the heavens, are the **LORD'S:** but the earth hath he given to the children of men.

<u>My prayer to activate, cultivate and transform my world:</u>

"Father, thank You for Your blessings of increase and multiplication. Please teach me to multiply what You have given me! I have seen Your faithfulness year after year and I know it is Your desire for me to increase. I break every strategy of the enemy and receive an abundance of revelation that leads to spiritual rewards, increase and multiplication. Increase me more and more, and my children. Today, I seek Your kingdom first, knowing that all things will be added unto me!"

Your Nugget for Today - 9

You Have Been Called To Live Beyond the Ordinary

ACT NOW! You have been called to live beyond the ordinary. In order to live this life, realize that the very life and power of Almighty God lives in you. You are filled with the same spirit that raised Christ from the dead! So let every demand of your time and strength be devoted to the growth and development of your relationship with Jesus Christ.

Serve God with humility and proclaim the message of Jesus Christ without fear. Be steadfast and unmoveable, always abounding in the work of the Lord. Never fear man but always fear God. Live a holy life and maintain a spirit of excellence in all things.

Repent from every mindset that does not agree with God's ways and God's Word. Bring every thought into captivity and make your thoughts obey God. Refuse to come into agreement with negativity. Come into agreement with the Word of God.

Let your heart and your words be in agreement with what God says about you. Let the very life of God shift your daily paradigm until you experience the manifestation of an extraordinary life. Be bold as a lion so the Lion of the tribe of Judah can form Himself in you. Yield to Holy Spirit so the extraordinary life can truly be yours.

Scripture Activation

2 Timothy:6-7

6 Wherefore I put thee in remembrance that thou stir up the gift of God, which is in thee by the putting on of my hands.

7 For God hath not given us the spirit of fear; but of power, and of love, and of a sound mind.

<u>My prayer to activate, cultivate and transform my world:</u>

"Father, thank You for this wonderful life You have called me to! Unite my heart to fear Your name. I repent from everything that does not line up with Your will for me. I break agreement with it. Live Your life through me. I'm created in Your image. Today I embrace boldness to live my extraordinary life."

Step Into the Destiny God Has for You

ACT NOW! Every day, you step into the destiny God has for you. God sees you wherever you are. Every day, you step into purpose.

God has called you by name at a strategic time in history. He has put you in a strategic place for His purposes. It does not matter what has happened to you in the past. You are here right now! You are valuable. You are needed. You are important to the Father.

Do not buy the lie that you are not needed. The Word of God tell us that every joint supplies. Not only do you need others, they need you! Your thigh bone cannot say to your knee, "I don't need you." We are all in the body together. Imagine a puzzle with only half of the pieces in place. You need all of the puzzle pieces to complete the picture.

God gave Nehemiah an assignment to rebuild the walls that had been torn down. Nehemiah needed every person in their place to complete the assignment. Because everyone was in place, functioning as God had called them to, they were able to complete the assignment in record time. You have an assignment in the earth. You have a prophetic destiny to fulfill and just as you need others, they need YOU to do the part God has called YOU to do.

Scripture Activation

Ephesians 4:15-16

15 But speaking the truth in love, may grow up into him in all things, which is the head, even Christ:

16 From whom the whole body fitly joined together and compacted by that which every joint supplieth, according to the effectual working in the measure of every part, maketh increase of the body unto the edifying of itself in love.

<u>My prayer to activate, cultivate and transform my world:</u>

"Father, I thank You that today, I step fully and without fear into the destiny You have for me. I step into Your purposes. I am valuable and needed for Your plans to be accomplished in the earth. I will fulfill my prophetic destiny."

You Are Called to Advance the Kingdom of Heaven

ACT NOW! You are called to advance the kingdom of heaven! When Jesus came to earth, he brought an ever-increasing kingdom. He did not bring a dead religion with no power. You are a citizen of this kingdom, called to live so close to the King, that you know the desires of His heart. His desires must become your desires.

Your number one priority must be to worship and serve the King and to reveal His will in the earth. Advancing the kingdom of heaven will require you to become more disciplined under His dominion. No more living day-to-day, not knowing your destiny or what God's progressive purpose is for your life. No more compromise, no more mediocrity, no more grumbling or complaining, no more settling for less than God's best for you! Time out for people, places and things that keep you from the will of God.

Being called by God to advance His kingdom is a privilege. Take what's yours by spiritual force, not natural force. Be a forceful worshipper, a forceful giver, a forceful forgiver. Be forceful in loving others. Be forceful in prayer and be forceful in reading God's Word.

It's time to make a shift from what you know to what He knows. You must expect higher, surrender higher, believe higher. This is your season of exponential growth. Purpose to connect with people of like belief, like surrender, like faith, those willing to go to the same level of sacrifice. The kingdom belongs to you. Take it by force!

Scripture Activation

Matthew 11:12
And from the days of John the Baptist until now the kingdom of heaven suffereth violence, and the violent take it by force.

<u>My prayer to activate, cultivate and transform my world:</u>

"Father, You have called me to advance Your kingdom in the earth. I'm finished with compromise and mediocrity. I forcefully give You my life so I can forcefully, by Your Spirit, take the kingdom by force."

God Wants to Enlarge Your Borders

ACT NOW! God wants to enlarge your borders. When Simon Peter heard the sound of the Word of God, his journey began. He then operated in obedience to the Word, not knowing that his borders and boundaries were being enlarged.

Peter was called with a miracle. When he received the call, he first looked at what had been. He said, "We have toiled all night, nevertheless at thy word..." Nevertheless, Peter considered the source. He thought about who was speaking to him and had a measure of expectation and faith that led to obedience and surrender to the Word. This is also our journey.

What Jesus did was bigger than what Peter had known in the past. Immediately, his levels were elevated. His journey began with a miracle of healing and a miracle of provision. What he did not know was that there would be a process to take him from here to there. From his miracles to his destiny. It all started with the sound of His voice. The sound of His voice brings change. When we are changed, we change others. As God showed His power to Peter, it was as if He was saying, "Peter, I am about to do something that will blow your mind, bigger than what you can handle!" The levels are being raised. Get ready for multiplication.

Scripture Activation

Luke 5:4-10

4 Now when he had left speaking, he said unto Simon, Launch out into the deep, and let down your nets for a draught.

5 And Simon answering said unto him, Master, we have toiled all the night, and have taken nothing: nevertheless at thy word I will let down the net.

6 And when they had this done, they inclosed a great multitude of fishes: and their net brake.

7 And they beckoned unto their partners, which were in the other ship, that they should come and help them. And they came, and filled both the ships, so that they began to sink.

8 When Simon Peter saw it, he fell down at Jesus' knees, saying, Depart from me; for I am a sinful man, O Lord.

9 For he was astonished, and all that were with him, at the draught of the fishes which they had taken:

10 And so was also James, and John, the sons of Zebedee, which were partners with Simon. And Jesus said unto Simon, Fear not; from henceforth thou shalt catch men.

My prayer to activate, cultivate and transform my world:

"Father, I say yes! I'm ready for You to enlarge my borders! I've toiled all night and have taken nothing. Nevertheless, at Thy word, I'm ready for multiplication!"

Your Nugget for Today -13

You Are Prophetic

ACT NOW! You are prophetic! You shall prophesy! The book of Acts tells us that in the last days, the sons and daughters of God shall prophesy. It doesn't say you might, it says you shall. According to Revelation 19:10, "The testimony of Jesus is the spirit of prophecy." That means that Holy Spirit who lives in you desires to testify of Jesus.

To prophesy means to speak under divine inspiration. It can mean to foretell an event or to forth tell a truth. 2 Corinthians 14 says the purpose of prophecy is to edify, exhort and comfort. To edify means to build up. To exhort means to encourage. To comfort means to console, support, reassure, cheer or bring relief from distress. Prophecy can also be that which is in agreement with what God has already spoken in His Word.

So take the Word of God in your mouth and begin to prophesy over your life each day. Say what God says. God says you are healed. God says you are free. God says you are victorious. God says eternal life is yours because you believe. God says He loves you. God says you are forgiven. God says joy is yours. God says He will be your Shepherd and lead you. God says He is your Deliverer. These are the last days. God is pouring out His Spirit. It's time to prophesy!

Scripture Activation

Acts 2:16-18

16 But this is that which was spoken by the prophet Joel;

17 And it shall come to pass in the last days, saith God, I will pour out of my Spirit upon all flesh: and your sons and your daughters shall prophesy, and your young men shall see visions, and your old men shall dream dreams:

18 And on my servants and on my handmaidens I will pour out in those days of my Spirit; and they shall prophesy.

<u>My prayer to activate, cultivate and transform my world:</u>

"Father, I thank You that I can speak Your Word and You will watch over it to perform it. I will see the prophetic fulfillment in my life! Thank You for pouring out Your Spirit upon me. I prophesy that by Your stripes, I am healed. I prophesy that greater is He that is in me than he that is in the world. I prophesy that because You love me, I am forgiven and the joy of the Lord is my strength."

You Can Live a Life of Revelation

ACT NOW! You can live a life of revelation. It's time to live in revelation, not only in information.

God, Who is Spirit, desires to reveal His secrets to those who fear Him. Daniel was one such person, who not only lived a life of excellence, but also a life of complete surrender to the plans and purposes of God. So much so, that favor was given to him and when he faced a difficult challenge, he knew beyond a shadow of a doubt that he would be victorious.

God loves to deliver us out of difficult situations as long as we don't bow to the ways of the world. Daniel didn't bow. He lived in such close communication with God that he lived a life of revelation. As a result, God revealed secrets to Daniel that ultimately shifted an entire government and set the course for his people.

Daniel literally prayed prophecy into fulfillment. God is no respecter of persons. Why not ask for the same spirit of excellence and surrender that led to a life of revelation?

Scripture Activation

Daniel 2:47
The king answered unto Daniel, and said, Of a truth it is, that your God is a God of gods, and a Lord of kings, and a revealer of secrets, seeing thou couldest reveal this secret.

<u>My prayer to activate, cultivate and transform my world:</u>

"Father, You Who reveals secrets, grant me revelation. I want to live a life of excellence. I want to live in such constant communication with You. I will not bow to the ways of this world. Let Your favor rest upon me and let Divine revelation be mine!"

Your Nugget for Today -15

You Are Complete in Him

ACT NOW! You are complete in Him! Complete means perfectly furnished and fully supplied.

When you move into a new home, it's not complete until you have it fully furnished. A partially furnished home won't do. Each room, from the living room to the dining room, to the bedroom must be equipped to serve your purposes. Even the kitchen must have all the supplies necessary to produce what's needed for sustenance. You are complete in Him. End of story.

Never shift into neutral because of others. Never listen to any voice that tells you what you cannot do. Stand in the strength and Spirit of God until His will is done. You are called and equipped. He has given you the supplies needed to fulfill any and every assignment.

Don't confine yourself to a soulish understanding of God, His truth, His Word and His will for your life. The Holy Spirit in you has the authority and the ability to do absolutely everything! You must see yourself, fully furnished and fully supplied in Christ.

Scripture Activation

Colossians 2:9-12

9 For in him dwelleth all the fulness of the Godhead bodily.

10 And ye are complete in him, which is the head of all principality and power:

11 In whom also ye are circumcised with the circumcision made without hands, in putting off the body of the sins of the flesh by the circumcision of Christ:

12 Buried with him in baptism, wherein also ye are risen with him through the faith of the operation of God, who hath raised him from the dead.

My prayer to activate, cultivate and transform my world:

"Father, I shout Hallelujah because I am complete in You! I have everything I need because I am fully furnished and fully supplied, ready to accomplish every good work You have called me to accomplish today and every day!"

You Are Dead, Yet Alive!

ACT NOW! You are dead, yet alive! There are no shortcuts to knowing God. We can only know Him through the cross, through His death, burial and resurrection.

Because God has given us free will, He asks us to choose: life or death. Take up your cross and follow Him. It will not always be comfortable.

Choosing your own will means not allowing His life to prevail in your life. Choosing His will means not allowing your life to remain. Identifying with the cross indicates that you have chosen God's life, not your own.

We must choose to die daily. Dead people don't have choices. They just obey. Dead people choose to always and only obey the will of God.

If you are truly dead to yourself, your own way is never a choice. A true disciple is one who adheres to the instructions of his master and makes that his only rule of conduct. We are to reckon ourselves to be dead to sin but alive to God. To reckon means to conclude or think. So this is the conclusion: you are dead, yet alive through Christ Jesus!

Scripture Activation

Romans 6:3-11

3 Know ye not, that so many of us as were baptized into Jesus Christ were baptized into his death?

4 Therefore we are buried with him by baptism into death: that like as Christ was raised up from the dead by the glory of the Father, even so we also should walk in newness of life.

5 For if we have been planted together in the likeness of his death, we shall be also in the likeness of his resurrection:

6 Knowing this, that our old man is crucified with him, that the body of sin might be destroyed, that henceforth we should not serve sin.

7 For he that is dead is freed from sin.

8 Now if we be dead with Christ, we believe that we shall also live with him:

9 Knowing that Christ being raised from the dead dieth no more; death hath no more dominion over him.

10 For in that he died, he died unto sin once: but in that he liveth, he liveth unto God.

11 Likewise reckon ye also yourselves to be dead indeed unto sin, but alive unto God through Jesus Christ our Lord.

<u>My prayer to activate, cultivate and transform my world:</u>
"Father, thank You for Your death, burial and resurrection so I can live. I say that I walk in newness of life. I choose obedience to Your will. Let Your life prevail in my life. I reckon myself to be dead to sin, but alive through Christ!"

ACT NOW!

Your Nugget for Today - 17

You Are a Sharp Instrument in the Hand of the Lord

ACT NOW! You are a sharp instrument in the hand of the Lord, able to thresh the highest, strongest and most stubborn enemy. To thresh means to separate grain with a flail or by the actions of a revolving mechanism. It's a violent or noisy movement, typically involving hitting something repeatedly.

God wants you to become a terror to those things that have been a terror to you. His Word says He will make you into this new instrument—new meaning fresh, rebuilt and repaired.

He will make you sharp—determined, eager and prepared, having teeth, meaning to have a two-edged sword. When the enemy comes, have no fear. You will crush, crumble, stamp, beat in pieces, bruise and make dust of the enemy with the Word of God. The enemy will be dispersed by the whirlwind. God will cause you to rejoice and spin around with exceeding great joy!

Scripture Activation

Isaiah 41:13-16

13 For I the **LORD** thy God will hold thy right hand, saying unto thee, Fear not; I will help thee.

14 Fear not, thou worm Jacob, and ye men of Israel; I will help thee, saith the **LORD**, and thy redeemer, the Holy One of Israel.

15 Behold, I will make thee a new sharp threshing instrument having teeth: thou shalt thresh the mountains, and beat them small, and shalt make the hills as chaff.

16 Thou shalt fan them, and the wind shall carry them away, and the whirlwind shall scatter them: and thou shalt rejoice in the **LORD**, and shalt glory in the Holy One of Israel.

My prayer to activate, cultivate and transform my world:

"Father, I rejoice in You! Because You make me a new, sharp, threshing instrument having teeth, the enemy is crushed and crumbled. I will now be a terror to those things that have tried to terrorize me."

You Were Made for Glory

ACT NOW! You were made for glory. I was made for glory. It is a gift from God. Glory is the inheritance of every believer. The word glory is defined as weight, splendor, copiousness, honor or honorable.

Only God has true glory. His glory shines brighter than the sun. Psalm 8 tells us that God has crowned us with glory. Therefore, we are created to live in the glory of our God—to walk in the glory, talk in the glory and have our being in the glory of our God.

To be crowned means to be encircled, either for attack or protection. That means that we are always surrounded by His glory. His glory will protect us from enemy attack. This is the revelation we must both learn and live to see and experience the manifested, tangible glory of God that will not only change our hearts, but the hearts of everyone in our sphere of influence.

God created man for His glory. Isaiah 43:7 says, "Even every one that is called by my name: for I have created him for my glory, I have formed him; yea, I have made him." Once we are yielded instruments, He can release His glory. In His glory, there is no lack. Healing, deliverance, joy, salvation, provision will all be released as we live in His glory. His glory not only shifts things, it transforms everything it touches.

Scripture Activation

Psalm 8:1-9

1 A Psalm of David. O LORD our Lord, how excellent is thy name in all the earth! who hast set thy glory above the heavens.

2 Out of the mouth of babes and sucklings hast thou ordained strength because of thine enemies, that thou mightest still the enemy and the avenger.

3 When I consider thy heavens, the work of thy fingers, the moon and the stars, which thou hast ordained;

4 What is man, that thou art mindful of him? and the son of man, that thou visitest him?

5 For thou hast made him a little lower than the angels, and hast crowned him with glory and honour.

6 Thou madest him to have dominion over the works of thy hands; thou hast put all things under his feet:

9 O LORD our Lord, how excellent is thy name in all the earth!

My prayer to activate, cultivate and transform my world:

"Father, thank You for creating me for Your glory! Thank You for crowning me with glory that protects me from enemy attack. I live and have my being in Your glory. I say that wherever I go, the glory of God goes and releases transformation. How excellent is Your name in my life! How excellent is Your name in my family. How excellent is Your name in all the earth!"

You Can Expect the Unexpected!

ACT NOW! You can expect the unexpected! There is a suddenly for you! Praise will release your suddenly!

In the story of Paul and Silas, we see two people who had been placed in prison because of their faith in Jesus Christ. They could have taken this opportunity to grumble or complain or even ask, "Where is God?" Being in prison might seem very much out of the will of God, but we can learn a valuable lesson from Paul and Silas.

When we find ourselves in a tight place, perhaps God is simply waiting to hear our praises! Then suddenly, not only will He show up, He will come and bring a suddenly that will shake the very foundation of that which tried to hold us captive!

All the doors will be opened! Doors of peace. Doors of hope. Doors of joy. Doors of healing. Doors of salvation. Doors of new opportunities. Doors of wealth. Doors of strength. Doors that will lead to your amazing destiny.

So expect the unexpected. Only believe that unexpected blessings will take place. Unexpected visitations from angelic beings will take place. Unexpected manifestations of the gifts of the Holy Spirit will take place. Unexpected signs and wonders will take place. Unexpected opportunities will present themselves. Praise God for the unexpected!

Scripture Activation

Acts 16:25-26

25 And at midnight Paul and Silas prayed, and sang praises unto God: and the prisoners heard them.

26 And suddenly there was a great earthquake, so that the foundations of the prison were shaken: and immediately all the doors were opened, and every one's bands were loosed.

My prayer to activate, cultivate and transform my world:

"Father, thank You for the unexpected! Thank You for the suddenly! Right now, I praise You! I thank You for shaking old foundations and opening doors for me! I shout hallelujah! I believe and I expect the unexpected!"

ACT NOW!

Your Nugget for Today - 20

God Will Open
New Doors for You

ACT NOW! God will open new doors for you. In order for God to open new doors, let Him set a watch and keep the door of your lips so you can access the door of heaven and pull down the blessings that you have been waiting for.

A door is an entryway, a gate or an opening. We think of doors being vertical. Entering into the door to your house can protect you from a storm. Doors can also be horizontal. Getting into your car requires you to enter a different type of door that can take you from where you are to a job interview that can change your life. Ask God to open the door of revelation that is linked to your destiny.

You must also know when to close a door. Close the doors of your ears. Never listen to the final word on any situation. God alone has the final word! Close the door to negative thinking. Don't come into agreement with lack, iniquity, defeat, reproach from the past, unbelief, condemnation or fear.

Keep the door open to love, joy, peace, long-suffering, gentleness, goodness, faith, meekness, humility and temperance. It's your words that open and close any door. Jesus tells us that His words are spirit and life! Prophesy His words and see the doors open!

43

Scripture Activation

Psalm 141:1-4

1 A Psalm of David. LORD, I cry unto thee: make haste unto me; give ear unto my voice, when I cry unto thee.

2 Let my prayer be set forth before thee as incense; and the lifting up of my hands as the evening sacrifice.

3 Set a watch, O LORD, before my mouth; keep the door of my lips.

4 Incline not my heart to any evil thing, to practise wicked works with men that work iniquity: and let me not eat of their dainties.

My prayer to activate, cultivate and transform my world:

"Father, keep the door of my lips. I want to see every door open for me that You desire. Help me to order my conversation in such a way that my words will please You and be acceptable in Your sight. Lord, let me see my open doors so I can have access to my future and receive the best that You have for me. I confess with my mouth that God's doors will be open to me and I say that I now shut all negative doors."

ACT NOW!

Your Nugget for Today - 21

God's Love Lives in You

ACT NOW! God's love lives in you. Because God, Who is love, lives in you, purpose in your heart to walk in love with one another.

In Matthew 18:15, Jesus explains to us not to hold a grudge or bitterness against a brother or sister. Go to that person so they can be given a chance to get things right with you and you can both be reconciled. We must realize that we have an enemy and he delights in bringing division and misunderstanding between those who God has called you to connect with. Holding grudges can destroy churches, ministries, friendships and families.

Remember, we are not fighting with flesh and blood. We are fighting principalities, powers, and spiritual wickedness in high places. These forces want nothing more than to destroy you, your family and your friends because we represent the image of God and the victory of Christ Jesus.

The truth is that the enemy has no power unless he can find a willing vessel to work through. Guard your heart. If someone hurt you, go to them and talk with them. Forgive one another so you don't give the enemy a foothold in your life. Don't hold a grudge. Always remember that God is love and He has called you to live a life of love.

Scripture Activation

I John 4:7-12

7 Beloved, let us love one another: for love is of God; and every one that loveth is born of God, and knoweth God.

8 He that loveth not knoweth not God; for God is love.

9 In this was manifested the love of God toward us, because that God sent his only begotten Son into the world, that we might live through him.

10 Herein is love, not that we loved God, but that he loved us, and sent his Son to be the propitiation for our sins.

11 Beloved, if God so loved us, we ought also to love one another.

12 No man hath seen God at any time. If we love one another, God dwelleth in us, and his love is perfected in us.

My prayer to activate, cultivate and transform my world:

"Father, show me if I am holding a grudge that I'm not aware of. Help me walk in forgiveness and to release all grudges. I will not hold on to it. I will let it go. I say, "Not on my watch!" Give me a revelation of Your love for me so I can allow You to love others through me. Let me be known as one who has fervent love for others. Your love dwells in me and is perfected in me."

You Are Resilient

ACT NOW! You are resilient. Isaiah 40:31 says that if we wait on the Lord, our strength will be renewed.

When we look at the word wait, it means to bind together by twisting. It is like the twisting together of two ribbons. As you twist them, they are no longer two separate pieces but they become one. That is what it means to wait on the Lord... to bind together and become one with Him. We are to bind together with Him in prayer and wait on Him in worship. He says if we do this, He will renew our strength, which means He will cause us to start again.

God is saying, "Put your trust and hope in Me. I will make you resilient." To be resilient means to spring back in shape and to recover quickly from difficulties. It is the ability and power to become strong, healthy, and successful after something bad or negative has happened. It means to withstand stress and respond with a bounce in your step—to respond with endurance and success.

We can begin again. He will cause us to return back to our original place of strength, of might, and ability. The word strength also means substance and wealth. Wait on the Lord for strength. Wait on the Lord for peace. Wait on the Lord for wealth strategies. Wait on the Lord for joy. Wait on the Lord the manifestation of your blessing. Don't be discouraged. Resilience is yours. Believe it, receive it, embrace it.

Scripture Activation

Isaiah 40:28-31

28 Hast thou not known? hast thou not heard, that the everlasting God, the LORD, the Creator of the ends of the earth, fainteth not, neither is weary? there is no searching of his understanding.

29 He giveth power to the faint; and to them that have no might he increaseth strength.

30 Even the youths shall faint and be weary, and the young men shall utterly fall:

31 But they that wait upon the LORD shall renew their strength; they shall mount up with wings as eagles; they shall run, and not be weary; and they shall walk, and not faint.

My prayer to activate, cultivate and transform my world:

"Father, I thank You for giving me power and for increasing my strength. I purpose to spend time with You, waiting in Your presence, binding together with You. I am ready to fly and I will soar higher and higher."

You Are Led by the Spirit of God

ACT NOW! You are led by the Spirit of God, therefore you are a son of God. There is a line being drawn in the spirit realm.

Until now, people have done anything and called it church. My father used to make stew. He would pull all the leftovers from the day before out of the refrigerator, put them in a pot and call it stew. But God says, "No more stew church, the true church will now emerge." He is calling for the true, spotless bride to arise. Those who will have ears to hear, obey and lay aside every weight.

God is looking for those who will allow Holy Spirit to consume them with His fire. Those who walk in this realm of the Spirit are those who can be assured that the gates of hell will not prevail against them.

Notice that the Scripture does not say the children of God, it says the sons of God. When we are born into the family of God, we are children and we will always be His children. As we continue to abide in Him, we grow into sonship. That means we grow in Him, being conformed to His image. You don't trust your car keys to your children until they have grown and matured and are able to walk in obedience to your authority. Be led by His Spirit. Let the sons of God arise!

Scripture Activation

Romans 8:11-14

11 But if the Spirit of him that raised up Jesus from the dead dwell in you, he that raised up Christ from the dead shall also quicken your mortal bodies by his Spirit that dwelleth in you.

12 Therefore, brethren, we are debtors, not to the flesh, to live after the flesh.

13 For if ye live after the flesh, ye shall die: but if ye through the Spirit do mortify the deeds of the body, ye shall live.

14 For as many as are led by the Spirit of God, they are the sons of God.

<u>My prayer to activate, cultivate and transform my world:</u>

"Father, thank You for calling me Your son. Holy Spirit, thank You for leading me. Help me to abide in You so I can continue to grow and be conformed into the image of Your Son, Jesus Christ. I say that I will arise and represent You as part of the true church against whom the gates of hell will not prevail!"

You Can Have a Renewed Spirit

ACT NOW! You can have a renewed spirit. When David, the man after God's heart, sinned again God, David made the right choice. He chose to cry out to God, asking Him to create in him a clean heart. Psalm 51:10 says, "Create in me a clean heart, O God; and renew a right spirit within me."

To create is something only God can do. It means to make something entirely new, not to remake something that already exists. David needed a new heart, one that would not even consider the thought of sinning against God. David wanted a new heart with new desires. He asked God to renew, repair and rebuild His spirit. He knew this would be the only way he would be able to have a "right" spirit within him. A "right" spirit is one that is upright and faithful.

Daily, we are tempted in many areas, tempted to yield to the desires of the world, the flesh and the devil. We can pray as David did, asking God for a clean heart—asking God to renew a "right" spirit inside of us so that doing His will at all times and having the love of the Father in us will be the thing we desire most. Let Him create in you a clean heart.

Scripture Activation

1 John:15-17

15 Love not the world, neither the things that are in the world. If any man love the world, the love of the Father is not in him.

16 For all that is in the world, the lust of the flesh, and the lust of the eyes, and the pride of life, is not of the Father, but is of the world.

17 And the world passeth away, and the lust thereof: but he that doeth the will of God abideth for ever.

<u>My prayer to activate, cultivate and transform my world:</u>

"Father, create in me a clean heart. Renew a right spirit within me. Let Your love abide in me so that doing Your will is what I desire most each day. Thank You for creating in me an upright and faithful heart."

ACT NOW!

God Has a Restoration of All Things for You

ACT NOW! God has a restoration of all things for you. Let us understand that within the kingdom, there is the law of restoration so we don't have to live beneath our privileges and delegated authority. In His Word, God promises to restore ALL things.

Joel 2 speaks of God's restoration. That which came to destroy and eat up your blessings, God says, "I will restore." Cry out for restoration. Cry out to recover all. God says, "I can restore what you have lost."

Complete restoration will come to your years—not just days or months, but years that the enemy has stolen. I studied every place that God mentioned restoration in the Bible. God says, "I will restore: health, lands, cities, finances, relationships, marriages, life, even life from the dead!" Those things that seem to have no life, God can and will restore: comforts, possessions, paths to dwell in Shalom (peace), your position in life... He will restore anything related to your soul, your spiritual renewal, your joy, your peace of mind, even an appetite for His Word. God can DOUBLE what was lost.

There is a law of restoration. Step into it. Remember, if something is taken it has to come back sevenfold. Call it back!! Shout, "RESTORE ALL THINGS!" Just because you don't see restoration take place overnight doesn't mean restoration is not coming. It doesn't mean God is not working! You must be restored so you can take restoration to your family, your friends, your nation, and the world.

ACT NOW!

The whole earth is waiting for the revelation of the SONS OF GOD. They are waiting for His royal Priesthood to arise… Waiting for HIS chosen generation, HIS holy nation to arise! God has made you to be a force in the earth, a carrier of His glory. An army with ability. A strong soldier with power, riches, substance and strength. The kingdom of God is here NOW! Step into restoration!

Scripture Activation

Joel 2:25-29

25 And I will restore to you the years that the locust hath eaten, the cankerworm, and the caterpiller, and the palmerworm, my great army which I sent among you.

26 And ye shall eat in plenty, and be satisfied, and praise the name of the LORD your God, that hath dealt wondrously with you: and my people shall never be ashamed.

27 And ye shall know that I am in the midst of Israel, and that I am the LORD your God, and none else: and my people shall never be ashamed.

28 And it shall come to pass afterward, that I will pour out my spirit upon all flesh; and your sons and your daughters shall prophesy, your old men shall dream dreams, your young men shall see visions:

29 And also upon the servants and upon the handmaids in those days will I pour out my spirit.

My prayer to activate, cultivate and transform my world:

"Father, thank You for the law of restoration at work in my life NOW! Thank You for restoring losses and revealing Your glory in the midst of restoration. I activate the law of restoration over my life! Let the restoration process manifest NOW!"

Your Nugget for Today - 26

You Are Filled with CHAYIL Power

ACT NOW! You are filled with CHAYIL power. Proverbs 31 speaks of the virtuous woman. She is a wise businesswoman who speaks with kindness, fears the Lord and takes care of her household.

The word for virtuous is the word CHAYIL. CHAYIL is a Hebrew word, meaning a force, an army, wealth, virtue, valor, strength, ability, activity, goods, host, might, power, riches, strength, strong, substance, valiant, virtuous, war, worthy. That's who you are! The power of God is working mightily in you each day to produce His CHAYIL power in you and through you.

CHAYIL is also the word for valor. Gideon was called a mighty man of valor. It didn't matter that the enemy was pressing in hard against him. It didn't matter that he didn't feel strong or powerful. It didn't even matter that he didn't realize the ability God had put in him. God called him a mighty man of valor. Whatever God says about you is who you are. Gideon led his people to victory. They conquered their enemies! Why do you need CHAYIL power?

A. **Your gates will be open to receive the harvest.** "Therefore thy gates shall be open continually; they shall not be shut day nor night; that men may bring unto thee the forces (CHAYIL) of the Gentiles, and that their kings may be brought." - Isaiah 60:11

B. **You will be continually strengthened.** "It is God that girdeth me with strength (CHAYIL) and maketh my way perfect." - Psalm 18:32

C. It qualifies you for service in the house of the Lord.
"Moreover thou shalt provide out of all the people able (CHAYIL) men, such as fear God, men of truth, hating covetousness; and place such over them, to be rulers of thousands, and rulers of hundreds, rulers of fifties, and rulers of tens: And let them judge the people at all seasons."
- Exodus 18:21-22

D. You will have power to get wealth to establish God's covenant. "But thou shalt remember the LORD thy God: for it is he that giveth thee power to get wealth (CHAYIL), that he may establish his covenant which he sware unto thy fathers, as it is this day." - Deuteronomy 8:18

E. You will be able to posses the land and your promises will manifest. You must war for your promises, war for your destiny, war for your future, war for your prophetic promises. "And I commanded you at that time, saying, The LORD your God hath given you this land to possess it: ye shall pass over armed before your brethren the children of Israel, all that are meet for the war (CHAYIL)." - Deuteronomy 3:18

Scripture Activation

2 Samuel 22:33
God is my strength and power (CHAYIL): and he maketh my way perfect."

<u>My prayer to activate, cultivate and transform my world:</u>
"Father, Jehovah CHAYIL, thank You that You created me to be a CHAYIL woman/man. You have placed Your CHAYIL power, strength, ability and wealth within me. Now I'm ready to go forward and posses the land You have promised me, accomplish any task, defeat any foe and leap over any wall. I'm qualified to serve You and I'm filled with wealth for the purpose of establishing Your kingdom. CHAYIL!"

The Throne Attitude is Yours!

ACT NOW! The throne attitude is yours! After Jesus conquered sin and death and rose from the dead, He returned to the Father. The Father said, "Sit at My right hand, till I make Your enemies Your footstool." So, the throne attitude of Jesus is to sit and expect His Father to bring all His defeated enemies under His feet.

We need a throne attitude like God Himself! He is telling us to have the same throne attitude as Jesus—sit, while He makes our enemies our footstool. All things, including the defeated enemies of disease, poverty, depression and all kinds of curses, are under our feet. The throne attitude will enable us to see from our seated position, in heavenly places with Him. Sitting implies resting. God says rest from striving, rest from trying to figure it out on your own. We will no longer see from our "condition" on earth.

To sit at the right hand of an earthly king was a place of honor, a place of special trust and authority because of the relationship with the king. It was something that was understood without needing explanation at the time. If you sat at the right hand of the king, it meant that you acted with his authority. Those who came to you would treat you with respect and obedience, as if you were the king himself.

ACT NOW!

In biblical times, defeated enemies were brought back in chains and the victorious king would sit on his throne and put his feet upon the necks of his defeated enemies as a sign of victory. Likewise, Jesus' conquered enemies are being dragged to Him one by one, and put under His feet. Rest from your labors. Enter into a place of rejoicing and praise. Rest in His finished work. Throne attitude!

Scripture Activation

Psalm 110:1-2
1 A Psalm of David. The LORD said unto my Lord, Sit thou at my right hand, until I make thine enemies thy footstool.
2 The LORD shall send the rod of thy strength out of Zion: rule thou in the midst of thine enemies.

My prayer to activate, cultivate and transform my world:

"Father, thank You that I am seated with You in heavily places. Help me to always see from my position, not my condition."

You Are a Force in the Earth!

ACT NOW! You are a force in the earth! God is looking for willing people who will say without hesitation, "We will do what you ask of us. We are willing." Willing to do what? They shall be willing while others are unwilling.

> **Willing** to voluntarily consecrate themselves for the service of the King.
> **Willing** to not be afraid to ask God what is on His heart, then volunteer to do it.
> **Willing** to lay hands on sick.
> **Willing** to cast out demons.
> **Willing** to go to the nations.
> **Willing** to be a voice against human trafficking.
> **Willing** to open a business.
> **Willing** to minister His love to prostitutes.
> **Willing** to go into prisons.
> **Willing** to adopt children.
> **Willing** to build orphanages.
> **Willing!**

And because they are willing, God will beautify them with salvation, because there is nothing in them to hinder His working. They will be a wise, strong, powerful people, led by the Spirit of God, able to rule in the midst of their enemies. They shall be willing in the day of His power. The word power is the word CHAYIL, meaning a force, an army, wealth, virtue, valor, strength, ability, activity, goods, host, might, power, riches, strength, strong, substance, valiant, virtuous, war, worthy.

This is the day of His CHAYIL power and God is calling for the willing ones to rise up and be His force in the earth. Within you is wealth, strength, ability, power and riches. We each have this treasure in our earthen vessel. Let's use it to change the world.

The same spirit that raised Jesus from the dead dwells in you. I am one of the "willing ones," are you? Let your commitment to God shape your under- standing. Don't let your understanding of God shape your commitment.

If you try to understand it all, you will never commit to be willing. This "willingness" is the essence of holiness; it constitutes "the beauties of holiness"—the beauty of Christ is released through His willing ones. This is the day of His CHAYIL power. It shall be seen in His willing ones.

Scripture Activation

Psalm 110:3
Thy people shall be willing in the day of thy power, in the beauties of holiness from the womb of the morning: thou hast the dew of thy youth

<u>My prayer to activate, cultivate and transform my world:</u>

"Thank You for making me a force in the earth. Thank You for your CHAYIL power! I am a willing one! I consecrate myself to Your service. Here am I, send me!"

If You Can See It, You Can Have It!

ACT NOW! If you can see it, you can have it! God told Abraham to lift up his eyes and look. The land that he could see would be given to him and to his descendants. He then instructed him to walk through the land that he saw.

Abraham, our father of faith, is our spiritual example. Faith is the substance of things hoped for, the evidence of things not seen. Our faith gives us eyes to see what our heavenly Father wants us to receive.

We can have what we see because of who HE is that has promised. Lift up your eyes. Look. What do you see? Contend by faith for the promises that you see.

We need faith. We can't please God without it. The children of Israel stayed in the wilderness because of unbelief. Don't let unbelief keep you from seeing your promises. Faith smiles at impossibilities.

Galatians 3 tells us that Abraham believed God and it was accounted to him for righteousness. It goes on to say that those who are of faith, the same are the children of Abraham. The kingdom of God operates by faith. If you can see it you can get it.

ACT NOW!

Remember, your feet can't go where your mind or your desire has not gone. According to your faith, it shall be. What do you desire? The just shall live by faith!

Scripture Activation

Genesis 13:14-17

14 And the LORD said unto Abram, after that Lot was separated from him, Lift up now thine eyes, and look from the place where thou art northward, and southward, and eastward, and westward:

15 For all the land which thou seest, to thee will I give it, and to thy seed for ever.

17 Arise, walk through the land in the length of it and in the breadth of it; for I will give it unto thee.

My prayer to activate, cultivate and transform my world:

"Father, increase my faith where it may be weak. Let my faith eyes see all that You have for me. Let me never shrink back in fear or unbelief but let me arise and possess the land. If I can see it, I can have it! I see it! It's mine because God said so. I live by faith!"

You Are Anointed to Fulfill a Specific Purpose in God's Plan

ACT NOW! You are anointed to fulfill a specific purpose in God's plan. So was Zerubbabel. Zerubbabel's name meant anointed to overflow.

He was commissioned to work with God on a project. He needed a miracle. First, he led those who were in captivity, back home. They returned with the gold and silver that had been stolen from them. Then, they started to rebuild the temple.

Although they were in obedience to God, they faced so much opposition that the building project stopped. Nevertheless! God spoke to him. He told him that He would help them and would crumble every mountain of opposition. So they started again and the assignment was completed.

Zerubbabel's story is proof that God's might and power will help you. It is never easy to achieve great accomplishments, and sometimes even in simple things opposition and difficulties come. Be encouraged. God's might and power will help you.

God will go before you to level all your mountains of opposition. By His power your circumstances can turn around in one day. By His power the impossible becomes possible. By the power of God, the impossible becomes possible. Say yes to God's plans, no matter what opposition you may face. Get ready to work with God as He works through you to accomplish His purpose.

Scripture Activation

Zechariah 4:6-10

6 Then he answered and spake unto me, saying, This is the word of the LORD unto Zerubbabel, saying, Not by might, nor by power, but by my spirit, saith the LORD of hosts.

7 Who art thou, O great mountain? before Zerubbabel thou shalt become a plain: and he shall bring forth the headstone thereof with shoutings, crying, Grace, grace unto it.

8 Moreover the word of the LORD came unto me, saying,

9 The hands of Zerubbabel have laid the foundation of this house; his hands shall also finish it; and thou shalt know that the LORD of hosts hath sent me unto you.

10 For who hath despised the day of small things? for they shall rejoice, and shall see the plummet in the hand of Zerubbabel with those seven; they are the eyes of the LORD, which run to and fro through the whole earth.

My prayer to activate, cultivate and transform my world:

"Father, I know that You have destined me for a specific purpose. You have commissioned me just as you called Zerubbabel. Thank You for going before me to level all mountains of opposition. I say yes to the plans You have for me, no matter what opposition I may face. I say that all impossibilities become possible. Work through me to accomplish Your purposes."

You Can Have the Wisdom of God

ACT NOW! You can have the wisdom of God. In Paul's first epistle to the Corinthian church, he exposed two kinds of wisdom: man's wisdom and the wisdom of God. Paul warns Corinth of the dangers of man's wisdom as he encourages the church to follow after the wisdom of God.

James 3:17 speaks of God's wisdom as wisdom "that is from above." This wisdom comes from the mind of God. It is the way that God thinks and the way that God performs. He also describes the fruit that it will produce. God's wisdom is "first pure, then peaceable, gentle, and easy to be entreated, full of mercy and good fruits, without partiality, and without hypocrisy."

Jesus Christ, is the embodiment of all of these things. When we find Him, we find wisdom. If we lack wisdom, we only have to ask God. He giveth to all men liberally. However, the source of worldly wisdom is man. Man's wisdom finds its source in human intellect, human ideas, human reasoning and human philosophy. The Bible calls it "earthly, sensual, devilish."

God has wisdom for every situation. Let's not lean to our own understanding but acknowledge Him in all our ways, knowing that He will not only direct our path, but give us the wisdom we need.

Scripture Activation

James 1:5-8

5 If any of you lack wisdom, let him ask of God, that giveth to all men liberally, and upbraideth not; and it shall be given him.

6 But let him ask in faith, nothing wavering. For he that wavereth is like a wave of the sea driven with the wind and tossed.

7 For let not that man think that he shall receive any thing of the Lord.

8 A double minded man is unstable in all his ways.

James 3:13-18

13 Who is a wise man and endued with knowledge among you? let him shew out of a good conversation his works with meekness of wisdom.

14 But if ye have bitter envying and strife in your hearts, glory not, and lie not against the truth.

15 This wisdom descendeth not from above, but is earthly, sensual, devilish.

16 For where envying and strife is, there is confusion and every evil work.

17 But the wisdom that is from above is first pure, then peaceable, gentle, and easy to be intreated, full of mercy and good fruits, without partiality, and without hypocrisy.

18 And the fruit of righteousness is sown in peace of them that make peace.

ACT NOW!

<u>My prayer to activate, cultivate and transform my world:</u>

"Father, thank You for giving me Your wisdom that is from above. I ask for wisdom in belief and in full assurance of faith without wavering. By faith I receive wisdom for every situation; wisdom that is pure and peaceable."

CONCLUSION

"Let us hear the conclusion of the whole matter: Fear God, and keep his commandments: for this is the whole duty of man." - Ecclesiastes12:13

Now that you have received your 31 nuggets, what will you do now? Will you continue to move forward in revelation or will you go back to what you have always known? Will you **ACT NOW** and step into your new place?

These pages were designed for you to visit over and over until each nugget becomes part of who you are. Move from information to revelation, from glory to glory. Life is supernatural. As you continue to seek Him, new revelation will come. Let Him show you how to apply it to your life in ever-increasing measures.

The winds of change are blowing in every sphere of life. God's desire is for you to be powerful, influential, wealthy. He wants you to oversee the affairs of the nations, walking in the favor and wisdom of God. Continue to speak the Word of God over your life each day. You will be activated, your heart will be cultivated and your world will be transformed.

Loose yourself from low-level thinking. It's a trick of the enemy to keep your mind filled with things that don't edify or promote God's kingdom agenda. That's just where the enemy wants you—busy with things that don't matter. When you are busy with things that don't matter, you won't have time for things that really matter.

Going forward, how do you want to live your life each day? It's your choice. You make the choice concerning who you are. **ACT NOW!**

Scripture Activation

Deuteronomy 30:19-20

19 I call heaven and earth to record this day against you, that I have set before you life and death, blessing and cursing: therefore choose life, that both thou and thy seed may live:

20 That thou mayest love the **LORD** thy God, and that thou mayest obey his voice, and that thou mayest cleave unto him: for he is thy life, and the length of thy days: that thou mayest dwell in the land which the **LORD** sware unto thy fathers, to Abraham, to Isaac, and to Jacob, to give them.

<u>My prayer to activate, cultivate and transform my world:</u>

(Pray your own prayer to God, based on what you have learned throughout this book.)

How I Plan to ACTIVATE, CULTIVATE and TRANSFORM My World:

_____

_____

_____

_____

_____

_____

_____

_____

_____

_____

_____

_____

How I Plan to ACTIVATE, CULTIVATE and TRANSFORM My World:

_____

_____

_____

_____

_____

_____

_____

_____

_____

_____

_____

_____

How I Plan to ACTIVATE, CULTIVATE and TRANSFORM My World:

_____

_____

_____

_____

_____

_____

_____

_____

_____

_____

_____

_____

How I Plan to ACTIVATE, CULTIVATE and TRANSFORM My World:

_____

_____

_____

_____

_____

_____

_____

_____

_____

_____

_____

_____

PAMELA HARDY

Dr. Pamela Hardy is an ordained minister, a preacher and teacher of the Word of God. She received a Master of Fine Arts degree and a Doctor of Ministry degree from FICU in Merced, California. Pamela has danced on Broadway in New York City and performed in national and regional touring productions.

Dr. Hardy travels throughout the United States and abroad. God has sent her as an Ambassador to over 20 countries, including Scotland, Germany, Nicaragua, Panama, Ecuador, South Africa, Israel, Malaysia, England, Canada, Costa Rica, Mexico, Suriname, Fiji, Holland, Korea and throughout the Caribbean.

She serves as Vice President of Chayil Women International, a global network focused on empowering women and changing lives. She is also co-owner of Basar Publishing Company. BPC is devoted to publishing the good news of Jesus Christ through advancing the ministry of the arts. She is the author of "Let the Nations Rejoice, An Invitation to Dance" and is a contributing author for "Every Knee Shall Bow," a literary compilation of international voices speaking on the importance of the movement arts, as well as an inspirational book for women entitled, "Dream Again: Awakening The Dreamer Inside Of You."

Dr. Hardy is the host of Global Horizons, an Internet Program focused on worship in the nations, and founder of Eagles International Training Institute, a mentoring program for those in dance ministry. EITI has a presence in over 20 countries. She also gives apostolic oversight to the EITI International Business Institute, Prophetic School, Flag Institute, Prayer Institute, Mime, Leadership Institute, Company of Prophets, School of Worship, Mime Institute, Authors Institute, Pageantry Institute, EITI Torah School, Drama School, Technique Center, TEN (The Eagles Network – Worldwide) and EITI Children.

She serves in leadership with her husband Christopher at Kingdom Ambassadors Global Impact Center and is also a member at Glory of Zion International under Apostle Chuck Pierce.

The prophetic anointing that is on her life will bring an increase in vision and will challenge and motivate others to be released into destiny and purpose. She is the Founder and Director of **Set Free Evangelistic Ministries.**

Contact Information:
Phone: **214-402-9647**
Email: **drpamelahardy@aol.com**
Websites: **www.drpamelahardy.org** / **www.eaglesiti.org**